EYES FIXED, MIND LOST

EYES FIXED, MIND LOST

SCREEN TIME EPIDEMIC

Sunnie Skiles, M. D.

CITI OF BOOKS

CITIOFBOOKS, INC.
3736 Eubank NE Suite A1
Albuquerque, NM 87111-3579
www.citiofbooks.com
Hotline: 1 (877) 389-2759
Fax: 1 (505) 930-7244

Ordering Information:

Quantity sales. Special discounts are available on quantity purchases by corporations, associations, and others. For details, contact the publisher at the address above.

Printed in the United States of America.

ISBN-13:   Softcover   979-8-89391-736-9

                  eBook   979-8-89391-737-6

Library of Congress Control Number: 2025911818

TABLE OF CONTENTS

INTRODUCTION

A few years ago, I walked into an exam room for an 18-month Well exam. An 18-month well exam is a routine pediatric check-up to monitor a child's growth, development, and overall health. I witnessed something that stuck with me. A toddler, just learning to walk, was fixated on an iPhone. When her mother took it away for the exam, the child erupted into a tantrum, inconsolable without her screen. This moment was a wake-up call for me. After 35 years as a pediatrician, I had seen this problem too often: kids relying too much on screen time.

My name is Dr. Sunnie Skiles. I graduated from U.C. Davis School of Medicine in 1987. I completed my Pediatric residency in Phoenix, AZ, at Phoenix Children's Hospital and Maricopa Medical Center in a combined program. I then moved to Northern California, where I have practiced pediatrics for decades. Throughout these years, I've observed the effects of excessive screen time on kids.

The problem is apparent. Children and teens are spending more time on their devices than ever before, leading to issues like physical inactivity, social isolation, and disrupted sleep patterns. Even more concerning is the rising rates of anxiety and depression linked to excessive screen time. These devices, meant to connect us, create a generation that feels more isolated than ever.

The consequences are significant. Children are missing out on vital face-to-face interactions. They are becoming less physically active, which impacts their overall health. Their mental well-being is at risk, with many experiencing increased levels of stress and anxiety. The very fabric of family life is changing. Screens now often take precedence over shared activities and meaningful conversations.

This book addresses these issues. I want to give parents the knowledge and tools to reclaim their family time and help their children lead balanced, healthy lives. I want to offer practical solutions to reduce screen time, encourage meaningful interactions and bring families closer.

My vision for this book is to help families build stronger connections and healthier lifestyles. I plan to guide parents in creating an environment where technology is balanced with other enriching activities. This will help children develop better social skills, improve their physical health, and enhance their emotional well-being. The title, "Eyes Locked, Minds Lost; Screen Time Epidemic," reflects this mission. It highlights the urgent need to address the screen time crisis and its impact on our children.

This book is for parents concerned about how much time their children spend on screens. It is for those who have witnessed firsthand the tantrums, the sleepless nights, and the growing distance in family relationships. It is also for educators and caregivers who want to understand the broader implications of screen time and how to support healthier habits in children.

The following chapters will provide a comprehensive overview of the screen time epidemic. I will share the research highlighting the negative impacts of excessive screen use. I will share stories from my practice and insights from experts in child development. Each chapter will offer realistic strategies for reducing screen time and promoting healthier alternatives.

From setting screen time limits to encouraging outdoor play, these solutions are designed to be realistic and achievable for busy families.

I invite you to join me on this journey. Together, we can make a difference in our children's lives, creating a more balanced, connected, and healthy future. Let's reclaim our time, strengthen our family bonds, and help our children thrive in the digital and real worlds.

CHAPTER 1

Understanding the Screen Time Dilemma

O ne evening, during a routine check-up, a mother told me that her ten-year-old son had become so engrossed in video games that he often skipped meals and neglected his homework. His grades began to slip, and he became increasingly irritable. Despite her efforts to limit screen time, the boy's attachment to games remained unyielding. Like many others I've encountered, this story underscores the pervasive challenge of managing screen time in our modern world.

The Digital Age: A Double-Edged Sword

Technology has become a big part of our lives, offering easy access to information, entertainment, and connection with others. With a few taps, you can connect with family and friends across the globe, stream your favorite shows, or find answers to pressing questions. These devices serve as portals to a world of knowledge and social interaction for children and teens, often enhancing their learning experiences and social connections.

The benefits of technology are undeniable. Educational apps and online learning platforms can supplement classroom learning, offering personalized education tailored to each child's needs. Social media allows children to maintain friendships and build new ones, fostering a sense of community and belonging. Interactive games can enhance cognitive skills, improve hand-eye coordination, and teach problem-solving strategies. When used appropriately, technology can be a robust growth and development tool.

None of us can ignore the downside of screen overuse. Imagine your child feeling anxious or sad without knowing why. Studies show that too much screen time can be a hidden cause, increasing the risk of these feelings. Children who spend excessive time on screens are at a higher risk of developing physical health issues, such as obesity and eye strain. Furthermore, constant exposure to fast-paced digital media significantly impacts their attention spans, making it harder to focus on tasks that demand sustained concentration—source: Effects of Excessive Screen Time on Child Development

(https://www.ncbi.nlm.nih.gov/pmc/articles/PMC10353947/)

Consider the Johnson family. Their teenage son, Alex, became addicted to online gaming. He would play late into the night, often skipping meals and ignoring his schoolwork. His parents were at their wits' end, unsure how to break the cycle. They decided to take a multi-faceted approach to address the issue. First, they set strict screen time limits and enforced them consistently. They also encouraged Alex to participate in physical activities like joining a local soccer team.

Additionally, they sought the help of a therapist to address the underlying emotional issues contributing to his addiction. Over time, Alex's behavior improved significantly. He became more engaged in school, his mood stabilized, and his physical health improved.

The Johnson family's experience shows the double-edged nature of technology. While digital devices can offer great benefits, but their overuse can lead to significant challenges. It's important for families to find a balance, ensuring that their children reap the benefits of technology without falling prey to its pitfalls. By setting clear boundaries, encouraging alternative activities, and seeking professional help when needed, families can navigate the complexities of the digital age and foster healthier, more balanced lives for their children.

In the chapters ahead, we'll explore the screen time problem in more depth, with practical tips and expert advice to help you manage your child's screen use. Topics will include the effects on sleep and behavior, promoting physical activity, and boosting academic performance. This book aims to give you the tools to create a healthier digital environment for your family. Together, we can address the screen time epidemic and help our kids thrive both online and offline.

1.2 Screen Time and Sleep: The Hidden Connection

The glow of screens has become a common sight in bedrooms across the globe. Yet, few realize how this seemingly harmless habit can wreak havoc on our children's sleep. The culprit? Blue light. Screens emit this short- wavelength light affects melatonin, the hormone responsible for regulating sleep-wake cycles. Research shows that Blue light from screens tricks the brain into thinking it's still daytime, making it harder for children to fall asleep. This results in restless nights and tired mornings. The science is precise: screens and sleep are not a harmonious mix. (Source: How Blue Light Affects Kids' Sleep)

Sleep studies consistently show that children exposed to blue light before bed experience delayed sleep onset or increased sleep latency, meaning they take longer to fall asleep. Beyond just falling asleep, the quality of sleep also suffers. Children may have more fragmented sleep, waking up frequently throughout the night. This poor sleep quality can lead to daytime drowsiness, making it hard for them to stay alert and focused. Over time, these disruptions can accumulate, severely affecting a child's overall health and development.

The consequences of inadequate sleep are far-reaching. It is essential to get enough rest, without which children often exhibit increased irritability and mood swings in the short term. They may become more prone to emotional outbursts, making it difficult for parents to manage daily routines. Cognitive impairments are another immediate effect. Lack of sleep can hinder a child's ability to concentrate, solve problems, and retain information, leading to decreased academic performance. Over the long term, chronic sleep deprivation can contribute to serious health issues. Children may face an increased risk of obesity due to hormonal imbalances that affect appetite and metabolism. A weakened immune system is another possible outcome, making them more susceptible to illnesses.

Parents often share stories about how screen time affects their kids' sleep. One mother shared her struggles with her eight- year-old daughter, who regularly used her tablet before bed. Even with an early bedtime, the child woke up groggy and irritable, and complained of headaches. She had trouble waking up in the morning and was tired throughout the day.

Her sleep was often interrupted at night, and this lack of rest showed in her behavior. Teachers noticed her focus in class was slipping, linking it to sleep deprivation. This situation is common for many parents, highlighting the need for practical solutions.

To improve sleep, it's important to establish a no-screen rule at least an hour before bedtime is crucial for increasing melatonin levels naturally, preparing the body for sleep. Introducing calming bedtime routines can also make a significant difference. Reading a book together or listening to soft music can create a calm and relaxing space that helps make falling asleep easier. For those who find it challenging to eliminate screens, using apps or devices that filter blue light can help cut out some effects. These filters reduce the intensity of blue light, making it less disruptive to the sleep- wake cycle.

Another practical approach is creating a consistent bedtime routine. Regularity helps reinforce the body's internal clock. Encourage activities that are calming and free of screens, such as taking a warm bath or practicing gentle stretches. It's also beneficial to make the bedroom a tech-free zone. Keeping devices out of the bedroom can significantly reduce the temptation to use them and promote an environment dedicated to rest. If removing devices isn't feasible, consider dimming the screens and using night mode settings that reduce blue light emission.

By incorporating these strategies, parents can improve their children's sleep quality and overall well-being. Better sleep has a great impact, leading to improved mood, academic performance, and physical health. As we continue to navigate the digital age, understanding and reducing the effects of screen time on sleep is crucial for fostering a healthier, more balanced lifestyle for our children.

1.3 Behavioral Changes Linked to Screen Overuse

One of the most noticeable effects of too much screen time is a change in a child's behavior. Parents often notice that their child become more irritable and aggressive when their screen time is limited, leading to frequent tantrums and emotional outbursts. These behavioral changes can be frustrating and hard to manage. Imagine a parent trying to enforce a screen time limit only to be met with a full-blown meltdown. This scenario is all too common in households today. Children get used to the constant stimulation provided by screens, making any interruption feel unbearable. Over time, they prefer interacting with their devices instead of engaging in real-life social activities. This shift can lead to social withdrawal, making it harder for children to develop and maintain meaningful relationships.

The effect of constant exposure to fast-paced digital media on a child's attention span and focus is concerning. Screens are designed to grab and hold attention with quick changes in images and sound. This environment can make it increasingly difficult for children to concentrate on tasks that require longer focus, such as homework or reading. Studies have shown high screen time is line to reduced attention spans and increased hyperactivity. In classrooms, teachers often notice students who struggle to pay attention, frequently zone out, or require constant redirection. These children may find engaging with slower-paced, less stimulating activities challenging, impacting their academic performance and overall learning experience.

The link between screen overuse and mental health issues is another important concern. Statistics show a troubling rise in anxiety and depression rates among youth, with too much screen time identified as a major contributing factor. Children and teens who spend too much time on screens are more likely to feel lonely, isolated, and have low self-esteem. Psychological theories suggest social media encourages constant comparison and that a lack of meaningful offline interactions can worsen these feelings. The pressure to maintain a perfect online persona can cause anxiety, while not having enough face-to-face socialization can lead to depression. This complex relationship between screen time and mental health highlights the need for a balanced approach to digital media use.

Parents can take several steps to reduce these behavioral changes and promote healthier screen habits. Setting clear screen time limits and sticking to them is crucial. Consistency helps children understand and accept boundaries, reducing the likelihood of resistance and tantrums. Encouraging participation in extracurricular activities can provide alternative sources of stimulation and engagement. Sports, arts, and hobbies offer physical activity, creativity, and social interaction opportunities. It's also important to have open discussions about feelings and screen use. Creating a safe space for children to express their emotions and concerns can foster better communication and understanding. Parents can model healthy screen habits by limiting device use and prioritizing face-to-face interactions.

Understanding these behavior changes and their causes can help parents make better decisions about their children's screen time. By using practical strategies and keeping open communication, families can handle the challenges of the digital age and create a healthier, more balanced lifestyle for their children. The goal isn't to get rid of screens but to balance their use with other activities that support overall well-being.

1.4 The Decline of Physical Activity

Digital devices have unintentionally encouraged a more inactive lifestyle for kids. This change has serious effects on their physical health. As children spend more time on screens, they miss out on chances to move and exercise. This lack of physical activity increases the risk of obesity and cardiovascular issues. Studies show that children who spend too much time on screens are likely to develop unhealthy eating habits, often snacking while watching videos or playing games. The combination of little movement and poor diet can lead to weight gain and the early onset of heart-related problems. Additionally, prolonged sitting can cause musculoskeletal issues such as back and neck pain, which can persist into adulthood if not addressed early.

Their level of activity significantly influences physical development in children. When children are not moving enough, their motor skills development can be delayed. Running, jumping, and playing sports are crucial for developing coordination and balance. These activities are necessary for children to be able to handle basic physical tasks, impacting their confidence and willingness to participate in physical challenges. Furthermore, a lack of physical activity weakens bone and muscle strength. During the formative years, bones need regular stress from activities like jumping and running to grow strong. Similarly, muscles develop through resistance and movement. Without these, children are at risk for weaker bones and muscles, which can lead to issues such as fractures or muscular imbalances later in life.

Real-life examples from families highlight the decline in physical activity due to screen overuse. One mother expressed her frustration about her son, who preferred playing video games over joining his friends for outdoor soccer. Despite her encouraging him, he showed little interest in physical activities, leading to weight gain and a noticeable drop in his energy levels. Another parent talked about how her daughter, once an avid swimmer, lost interest in the sport as she became more engrossed in social media. The struggle to motivate kids to be active is a common theme among parents today. They find it challenging to compete with the instant gratification and endless entertainment that screens provide.

Parents can take practical steps to combat this decline in physical activity. Scheduling regular family exercise times can make a significant difference. Whether it's a weekend hike, a bike ride around the neighborhood, or even a dance-off in the living room, setting aside time for shared physical activities can encourage children to be more active. Another effective strategy is introducing fun physical activities that align with a child's interests. Sports, dance classes, or even martial arts can provide structured ways for kids to stay active and develop new skills. Limiting screen time as a reward for physical activity can also be a motivating factor. For instance, allowing extra screen time only after a certain amount of physical activity can create a balanced routine that prioritizes health.

These strategies promote physical health and offer opportunities for family bonding. Engaging in activities together strengthens family relationships and creates lasting memories. It's important to lead by example; children who see their parents valuing physical activity are more likely to adopt similar habits. By taking these steps, parents can help their children develop a healthier, more active lifestyle, balancing out the effects of too much screen time.

1.5 Academic Performance and Screen Time

In today's digital era, the impact of screen time on academic performance is a growing concern among parents and teachers. Studies consistently show too much screen time can significantly affect a child's learning. One common problem is the reduction in homework completion rates. Children who spend more time on screens often find it challenging to focus on their studies, leading to incomplete or poorly done assignments. This lack of focus carries over to the classroom, where the constant distraction of digital devices can result in lower test scores and grades. Teachers frequently report that students with high screen time struggle to pay attention, participate in discussions, and retain information, which are crucial for academic success.

Differentiating between productive and unproductive screen time is essential for parents aiming to support their children's learning. Productive screen time includes educational apps and programs that enhance learning and development. These tools can provide interactive and engaging ways for children to grasp complex concepts and reinforce classroom learning. For instance, apps that offer practice exercises in math or interactive science simulations can make learning more accessible and enjoyable. In contrast, unproductive screen time, such as playing video games or browsing social media, offers little to no educational value and can detract from time spent on more enriching activities. Research indicates that while educational digital tools can be practical, excessive entertainment media use often overshadows their benefits.

Parents' concerns about the impact of screen time on academic performance are valid. One mother shared how her son, who used to be an A-student, saw a significant drop in his grades after he became addicted to online gaming. She observed that he frequently procrastinated on his homework, choosing to play games instead. Despite her efforts to set limits, the lure of the virtual world was too strong. Teachers also noticed him paying less attention in class and not wanting to participate in group activities. Another parent shared how her daughter's addiction to social media resulted in late-night browsing sessions, leaving her too tired to concentrate on her studies the next day. These stories show how the real-world implications of unregulated screen time on children's academic performance.

Parents can use several strategies to help their children balance screen time with schoolwork. Creating a structured homework and screen time schedule can give children a clear routine to follow. Setting specific times for homework and screen use helps prioritize school tasks. Regular breaks and physical activity between study sessions can also improve focus. Short breaks for stretching or a quick walk can refresh the mind, making it easier for children to get back to their studies. Adding educational apps to support school learning can make study time more engaging. Apps with quizzes, flashcards, and interactive lessons can reinforce what children learn in class in a fun way.

By understanding the differences between productive and unproductive screen time and setting up structured routines and breaks, parents can help their children develop healthier screen habits that support their academic growth. The goal is not to eliminate screen time but to ensure that it is balanced with other essential activities that contribute to a child's overall development and success in school.

Social Skills in the Digital Era

In an age where screens dominate our children's lives, developing crucial social skills often takes a back seat. Excessive screen time can severely hinder a child's ability to engage in face-to-face interactions. Children become used to the digital world, where communication is often limited to text messages and emojis. This lack of real-world interaction can lead to difficulty reading social cues and body language. For instance, understanding subtle facial expressions or interpreting tone of voice are skills honed through in-person communication, essential for forming meaningful relationships. When children spend more time interacting with screens than with people, these abilities still need to be developed.

The impact of excessive screen time extends to relationships with both peers and family members. Children may begin to prefer online communication to in-person interactions. This change can strain relationships as the richness of face-to-face conversations is replaced with shorter, less meaningful digital chats. Family dynamics also suffer. Parents often find that meals, outings, and even simple conversations are interrupted by the constant presence of devices. Imagine a family dinner where everyone is more engaged with their screens than with each other. This distraction reduces the quality of family time and weakens the bonds crucial for a supportive and nurturing home environment.

The real-life consequences of this shift are clear in many families. One parent shared how her once outgoing and friendly daughter became increasingly isolated after getting her first smartphone. The child spent hours scrolling through social media, gradually withdrawing from family activities and losing interest in spending time with friends. This social isolation led to feelings of loneliness, affecting her emotional well-being. Another family noticed how their son's obsession with online gaming resulted in fewer family interactions. They noticed a drop in the quality of their conversations and a growing sense of disconnection. These stories show the real effects of screen time on social skills and relationships.

Parents can take several proactive steps to enhance their children's social skills. Encouraging participation in group activities and sports is a great start. These environments allow children to interact, collaborate, and build friendships. Setting up playdates and family gatherings can also foster social interactions. These events allow children to practice communication skills in a relaxed and enjoyable setting. Modeling good social behavior and communication skills is equally important. Children learn by observing their parents. Demonstrating active listening, maintaining eye contact, and showing empathy in conversations can set a positive example for them to follow.

By implementing these strategies, parents can help their children develop the social skills to navigate their digital and real-world environments. Encouraging real-life interactions over virtual ones can build stronger, more meaningful relationships. While technology offers many benefits, it's crucial to ensure that it doesn't come at the expense of essential social development. The goal is to create a balanced approach where screens and social skills coexist harmoniously, fostering well-rounded, emotionally healthy children who can thrive in any setting.

CHAPTER 2

Identifying and Addressing Common Pain Points

Imagine walking into your living room and seeing your child, eyes glued to a tablet, not paying attention to the world around them. You call their name once, twice, three times, but there's no response. When you finally get their attention and suggest putting the device away, they resist or maybe even have a meltdown. This is a common situation many parents face today. The daily battles over device use can be exhausting, leaving you feeling like a referee in your own home. To regain control, it's important to understand why children resist limiting screen time and how you can establish simple guidelines to reduce these conflicts.

Daily Battles Over Device Use

Understanding the Root Causes

Children often resist limiting screen time because of both psychological and social factors. One key reason is the desire for instant gratification. Digital devices are designed to provide quick rewards—whether it's a new high score in a game, a notification from a social media app, or the next episode of a favorite show. This instant gratification can become addictive, making it difficult for children to step away from their screens. They get used to the rapid feedback and stimulation, which can make real-world activities', with their slower pace, less appealing.

Another major factor is the fear of missing out, commonly known as FOMO. Social media platforms often heighten this fear by constantly updating users on what their friends are doing. Children and teens, in particular, are highly vulnerable to FOMO. They worry about missing important updates, events, or conversations if they step away from their devices. This anxiety can make it incredibly challenging for them to willingly disconnect, even temporarily.

Establishing Clear Guidelines

Setting clear and consistent screen time rules is essential to address this issue. Start by determining daily screen time limits based on your child's age. The American Academy of Pediatrics recommends that younger children have no more than one hour of screen time per day, not including educational use. Consider creating a family media plan to formalize these rules. This plan can outline when and where screens are allowed, what types of content are acceptable, and the consequences for breaking the rules. Involve your children in this process to give them a sense of ownership and responsibility.

Techniques to Reduce Conflict

Reducing arguments over screen time requires practical methods that make the transition smoother. One effective method is using timers and alarms to signal when screen time is over. This gives kids a clear, non-negotiable cue, making the transition easier and helping them mentally prepare to stop. Another strategy is creating a reward system for following the screen time rules. For example, children can earn "tech tickets" that allow them additional screen time as a reward for completing chores or homework. This system not only sets limits but also rewards behavior.

Examples from Real Life

Consider the Smith family, who introduced a "tech ticket" system for managing their children's screen time. Each child received a set number of tickets for screen time each week. If they wanted more time, they had to earn it by completing tasks or behaving well. This approach transformed the daily battles into a more manageable routine. The children learned to budget their screen time, leading to fewer conflicts.

The Johnson family also found success by using a points system. Each child earned points for following the screen time guidelines, which could be traded for rewards like a family outing or a special treat. This system helped manage screen time but also promoted a sense of achievement and cooperation within the family, resulting in fewer meltdowns and more engangement in other activities.

Understanding the root causes of resistance to screen time limits and setting up clear guidelines and practical techniques can transform daily battles into more peaceful interactions. These strategies can help your family create a balanced approach to screen use, promoting healthier habits and stronger relationships.

Managing Screen-Induced Tantrums

Recognizing what triggers tantrums is the first step to preventing them. One major trigger is sudden shift from screen time to other activities. Imagine your child deeply engrossed in a video game or a favorite show; then, suddenly, you ask them to stop and come to dinner. This abrupt change can be jarring and upsetting, leading to emotional outbursts. Stimulation from bright screens and fast-paced content also contributes to these meltdowns. The constant barrage of images and sounds can overwhelm a child's senses, making it challenging to cope with the natural world once the screen is removed.

To prevent these tantrums, try giving your child a five-minute warning before screen time ends. This heads-up allows children to mentally prepare for the transition, making it less abrupt and more manageable. Saying something like, "In five minutes, it's time to turn off the tablet and get ready for dinner, " can make a big difference. Another strategy is engaging children in calming activities post-screen time. Activities such as reading a book, drawing, or playing with sensory toys can help ease the transition from the overstimulating digital world to the calmer, real one.

When tantrums occur, having a set of calm-down techniques can be very helpful. Deep breathing exercises are a powerful tool to help children regain control over their emotions. Teach them to take slow, deep breaths: in through the nose, hold for a few seconds, and then out through the mouth. This practice can help lower their heart rate and reduce anger or frustration. Another effective method is creating a "calm down corner" with sensory toys like stress balls, fidget spinners, or soft blankets. This designated space allows children to retreat and self-soothe when they feel overwhelmed, providing them with the tools to calm down independently.

As a parent, It's important to stay calm and supportive during these tantrums. Avoid punishing your child, as this can make things worse and cause them to feel misunderstood. Instead, try to show empathy. Acknowledge their feelings by saying, "I see you're upset because it's time to turn off the TV. It's okay to feel that way, but we need to stick to our schedule." This approach validates their emotions while still reminding them of the rules. Reinforcing positive behavior with praise and rewards is also effective. When your child successfully steps away from the screen without a tantrum, acknowledge their effort. Simple phrases like, "Great job turning off the tablet without getting upset," can go a long way in encouraging positive behavior.

Recognizing these triggers and using these strategies can significantly help manage screen-induced tantrums. By preparing your child for transitions, providing calming activities, and showing empathy, you can lower how often and intensely these outbursts happen. This approach not only helps create a more peaceful home environment but also teaches your child important skills in emotional regulation and self-control.

Screen Time and Sleep Deprivation

The glow of screens in dark rooms is common in many homes, but this habit can really disrupt sleep patterns. One big reason for this is the blue light that screens give off. This light can block the production of melatonin, the hormone that helps regulate sleep. When children are exposed to blue light before bed, their bodies find it hard to make enough melatonin, making it tougher for them to fall asleep. This delay can lead to several problems, like struggling to wake up in the morning and having trouble focusing or experiencing mood swings during the day.

Engaging content also plays a big part in delaying bedtime. Whether it's an exciting video game, a captivating TV show, or scrolling through social media, children can get so caught up in what they're watching or playing that they end up staying up later than they should. The excitement keeps their brains active, making it hard for them to relax. This combination of stimulating content and blue light creates a perfect storm for sleep problems. As a result, children who go to bed late often have trouble getting quality sleep, even when they finally do fall asleep.

Creating a sleep-friendly environment can really help improve sleep quality. One effective way to do this is by removing all electronic devices from the bedroom. This helps eliminate the temptation to use screens right before bed and reduces the chances of sleep disruptions. Instead, you can introduce relaxing bedtime routines that signal to the body that it's time to wind down. Activities like reading a book, listening to soft music, or having quiet conversations can create a calm atmosphere that is good for sleep. Dimming the lights and making sure the room is cozy and comfortable can also enhance the sleep environment.

Setting a digital curfew is another effective strategy. Establishing a no-screen rule at least one hour before bed allows the body time to adjust and start producing melatonin naturally. During this time, encourage relaxing activities like reading a book or listening to soft music. These activities can help calm the mind and create a consistent bedtime routine that signals to the body that it's time to sleep. For younger children, incorporating a bedtime story can be especially helpful, providing a soothing transition from the day's activities to a restful night.

Families that use these strategies often notice significant improvements in their children's sleep. For instance, the Martinez family started a bedtime reading routine for their two kids, ages six and eight. Each night, the children would pick a book, and the family would spend 30 minutes reading together before bed. This small change made a big difference in the kids' sleep quality. They fell asleep more quickly, slept longer, and woke up feeling refreshed and alert.

Another success story comes from the Lee family, who created a "tech basket" for storing devices overnight. An hour before bedtime, everyone, parents included, had to put their phones, tablets, and laptops in the basket. This non- negotiable rule led to a significant decrease in nighttime screen use and a dramatic improvement in everyone's sleep quality. The children became more involved in their bedtime routines, and the parents noticed a calmer, more peaceful atmosphere in the evenings.

Identifying sleep disruptors and using practical strategies can greatly improve your child's sleep. By removing electronic devices from the bedroom, creating relaxing bedtime routines, and setting a digital curfew, you can make a sleep- friendly environment that encourages better rest. These changes not only enhance sleep quality but also boost overall well-being, helping your child wake up refreshed and ready for the day.

The Struggle to Balance Homework and Screen Time

Balancing homework and screen time is a common challenge for many families. Children often feel torn between the excitement of entertainment and the need to study, which can lead to distractions and procrastination. This conflict arises because screens provide instant gratification, while homework demands sustained effort and concentration. The bright colors, fast-paced content, and interactive nature of digital media are very engaging, making it hard for children to shift their focus to more challenging tasks like math problems or reading assignments. Many children also lack self-discipline and time management skills to prioritize their responsibilities effectively. This can result in delayed homework, rushed assignments, and frustration, which only adds to the problem.

Creating a structured routine can help ease the challenges of balancing homework and screen time by providing clear boundaries and expectations. Start by setting specific times for homework and screen use and establishing a daily schedule that includes designated study periods and breaks for screen time. Visual schedules or planners can be helpful, as they give children a tangible way to see and understand their daily commitments. For example, a chart on the refrigerator or a planner on their desk can remind them of their responsibilities. This structure aids in time management and reduces conflicts over screen use.

Enhancing focus and productivity is also important in achieving this balance. One effective method is the Pomodoro Technique, which breaks study sessions into 25- minute intervals followed by a 5-minute break. This approach makes study time feel more manageable and less overwhelming. Another key strategy is creating a dedicated, distraction-free study space. This area should be free from electronic devices, noise, and other distractions. A quiet corner of the house, equipped with necessary supplies like textbooks and notebooks, can significantly improve your child's ability to concentrate. Ensuring this space is exclusively for homework can help reinforce focused study habits.

Parental involvement is crucial in helping children balance screen time with academic responsibilities. Regular check-ins and progress monitoring can keep your child on track and provide opportunities for guidance and support. These check-ins can be as simple as asking about their day, reviewing homework assignments, and discussing any challenges they face. Setting clear expectations and offering positive reinforcement is also essential. Ensure your child knows what is expected of them regarding homework and screen time. When they meet these expectations, acknowledge their efforts and achievements. Praise or small rewards can motivate them to develop good habits.

Parents can also support their children by modeling effective time management and a balanced approach to screen use in their own lives. If children see you prioritizing your responsibilities and limiting your screen time, they are likely to adopt similar behaviors. Encouraging a family culture that values education, commitment, and balanced screen use can create an environment where children feel supported in managing their time effectively.

Balancing homework and screen time requires a comprehensive approach that addresses the underlying conflicts and provides practical solutions. By creating a structured routine, enhancing focus and productivity, and actively involving yourself in your child's academic life, you can help them develop the skills and habits needed to manage their screen time responsibly. This balance not only improves academic performance but also fosters a healthier relationship with technology, laying the groundwork for lifelong success.

Identifying Signs of Screen Addiction

Recognizing the signs of screen addiction in children is important for parents. One clear indicator is irritability when they aren't using screens. You may notice your child becoming agitated, restless, or even angry when asked to put down their device. This irritability can affect their mood and interactions with family members. Another significant sign is neglecting responsibilities. Children addicted to screens often lose interest in activities they once enjoyed. For example, a child who loved playing outside may now prefer staying indoors to play video games, neglecting homework, chores, and even personal hygiene in favor of screen time. This shift can be alarming and suggests that screen use has turned from a simple pastime into a compulsive need.

Assessing your child's screen time habits can offer valuable insights into whether they are developing an addiction. One effective method is to keep a screen time diary. This involves tracking how much time your child spends on different devices each day, noting the start and end times, the types of activities they engage in, and any changes in their behavior or mood. This diary can help identify patterns and triggers for excessive screen use.

Various apps are also available to track and limit screen usage, providing detailed reports on how much time your child spends on each activity. These tools can be eye-opening, revealing how much time screens consume in your child's daily routine. By understanding your child's screen habits, you can make informed decisions about managing and reducing screen time.

The impact of screen addiction on children's health and well-being is significant. One major consequence is increased anxiety and depression. Excessive screen time can lead to social isolation, as children spend more time interacting with devices than with people. This lack of real-world social interaction can contribute to feelings of loneliness and depression. Additionally, constant exposure to idealized images and lifestyles on social media can worsen anxiety and low self-esteem, causing children to feel inadequate or left out, which creates a cycle of negative emotions.

Declining academic performance is another serious impact. Children addicted to screens often struggle to concentrate on their studies, resulting in lower grades and decreased engagement in school. This academic decline can further affect their self-esteem and overall development, creating a challenging cycle to break.

Seeking professional help is a crucial step when screen addiction becomes overwhelming. Consulting a pediatrician can be a good starting point, as they can assess your child's overall health and provide tailored recommendations. A child psychologist can offer deeper insights into the emotional and psychological aspects of screen addiction. Therapy options like cognitive-behavioral therapy (CBT) can be particularly effective, helping children understand and change the thought patterns that drive their addictive behaviors. Support groups for both parents and children can also be beneficial, providing a platform to share experiences, gain support, and learn new strategies for managing screen time.

Recognizing the signs of screen addiction is the first step toward addressing the issue. Tools like screen time diaries and tracking apps can help assess your child's habits and identify areas for improvement. Understanding the impact of screen addiction on health and well-being highlights the importance of taking action. When necessary, seeking professional help can provide the guidance and support needed to help your child regain control over their screen use.

Through these efforts, you can help your child develop a healthier relationship with technology and ensure their overall well-being.

Dealing with Screen-Induced Mood Swings

You've likely seen how your child's mood can change drastically after spending too much time on screens. One minute they're happily focused on their device, and the next, they're irritable and uncooperative. This isn't just a coincidence; excessive screen time can lead to mood swings and emotional dysregulation for several reasons.

One major factor is overstimulation from screen content. Bright screens, rapid movements, and engaging visuals can overwhelm a child's sensory system. This sensory overload makes it hard for them to switch back to less stimulating activities, leading to frustration and mood swings.

Additionally, when children spend too much time on screens, they often neglect essential daily activities like meals, exercise, or sleep. This disruption can throw off their internal clock, making them more prone to emotional ups and downs. For example, if a child skips dinner because they're too wrapped up in a game, they might have a meltdown later due to hunger and fatigue. It's a cycle that can be tough to break.

To help children manage their emotions and reduce screen- induced mood swings, several strategies can be effective. Mindfulness and relaxation exercises are helpful; teaching your child simple techniques like deep breathing or guided imagery can calm them down when they feel overwhelmed. Encouraging outdoor play and physical activity is another great way to balance their emotional state. Physical activities release endorphins, the body's natural mood lifters, providing a healthy outlet for pent-up energy and stress.

Maintaining a healthy balance between screen use and emotional well-being is essential. Set limits on screen time and ensure regular breaks to prevent overstimulation. For example, establishing "no screens" during meals or an hour before bedtime can reset their emotional state and create space for other enriching activities. Promoting activities that foster emotional resilience—like journaling, drawing, or pursuing hobbies—can also be beneficial. These activities allow children to express themselves and process their emotions constructively.

Parental support and open communication are vital in helping children navigate their feelings. Regular family discussions about screen habits and emotions can provide a safe space for your child to share their experiences. Asking open-ended questions, such as "How do you feel after spending a lot of time on your tablet?" encourages them to express their thoughts. It's also important to model healthy screen use and emotional regulation. Children often mimic their parents, so showing them how to manage screen time and emotions effectively sets a positive example.

For instance, one family I worked with started incorporating daily walks into their routine. After dinner, they would leave their devices at home and take a 30-minute walk together. This simple activity provided exercise, family bonding, and emotional decompression, leading to a noticeable reduction in mood swings and improved emotional well-being.

Another parent established a "tech-free hour" after school. During this time, the family engaged in various activities like cooking, playing board games, or just talking about their day. This break from screens helped the children transition from the overstimulating school environment to a more relaxed home atmosphere. Over time, the children became more emotionally stable and less prone to mood swings.

Once identified, you can begin to address the issue by:

1. Using Techniques to help manage emotions.

2. Ensuring a balanced approach to screen use and emotional well-being.

3. Offer support from parents and encourage open communication.

These steps are designed to help your child develop healthier habits and achieve a more stable emotional state. The key takeaway is that small, consistent changes can lead to significant improvements in your child's overall well-being.

CHAPTER 3

Practical Strategies for Reducing Screen Time Creating Screen-Free Zones at Home

Creating Screen-Free Zones at Home

Imagine a typical evening at home. You gather your family for dinner, expecting some quality time together. However, instead of chatting, everyone's face is lit by the glow of screens- smartphones, tablets, and TVs have taken over the dinner table, disrupting the time for connection. This is something familiar for many families, but it doesn't have to be this way. By creating screen-free zones in your home, you can reclaim these precious moments and strengthen family bonds.

Screen-free zones are designated areas in your home where digital devices are not allowed. These spaces encourage face- to-face conversations and provide a break from the constant digital distraction. Common areas to consider for screen-free zones are the dining room and bedrooms. The dining room, often the hub family time, should be a space for uninterrupted conversations. Bedrooms, on the other hand, should be peaceful places for rest, free from the blue light that can disrupt sleep.

The benefits of creating screen-free zones go far beyond cutting down on screen time. One of the biggest advantages is better family communication and bonding. Family members are more likely to have meaningful conversations, share their thoughts and experiences, and strengthen their relationships without screens. This improved communication brings a sense of unity and support, making the home a more peaceful and connected place.

Better sleep quality and hygiene are other key benefits of screen-free zones. Keeping screens out of the bedroom can create an environment that promotes more restful sleep. Electronic devices can make staying awake late, scrolling through social media, or watching videos tempting. Limiting screen time, especially before bed, helps regulate sleep patterns, which in turn improves overall health and well-being. Additionally, screen-free zones can enhance focus and productivity in non-screen activities. Both children and adults may find it easier to concentrate on tasks like reading, studying, or enjoying creative hobbies without the constant distraction of digital devices.

Implementing screen-free zones in your home takes careful planning and open communication. Begin by identifying which areas should be screen-free, and involve your family in explaining why these spaces should be device-free. Including everyone in this decision-making process helps build a sense of ownership and cooperation. Once the zones are decided, set clear rules and make sure everyone understands their purpose and the expectations for maintaining them. Physical reminders, like signs or storage bins for devices, can help reinforce the rules and make them easier to follow.

Maintaining screen-free zones takes continuous effort and commitment. Regularly review and reinforce the rules to make sure they remain effective. Encourage fun family activities in these areas to make them inviting. For example, keep board games, puzzles, and cards easily accessible in the dining room to promote interactive play. Arrange seating to encourage conversation and interaction by placing chairs in a circle or around a cozy coffee table. Comfortable seating options, like pillows and bean bags, make these spaces more appealing for relaxation and socializing.

Sharing success stories can also inspire and motivate commitment to screen-free zones. Talk about how these zones have positively impacted your family's life through improved communication, better sleep, or more meaningful interactions. These stories can serve as a positive reminder of the benefits and motivate everyone to continue prioritizing screen-free time.

To make this transition smoother, try creating a visual checklist that highlights the benefits and rules of your screen- free zones. Place the checklist in a prominent spot, such as on the refrigerator or a bulletin board, where it can be a constant reminder. This visual aid can reinforce the importance of screen-free zones and keep the whole family aligned with the goals. Here's an example:

Screen-Free Zone Checklist

- **Benefits:**
  - ○ Improved family communication and bonding
  - ○ Better sleep quality and hygiene
  - ○ Enhanced focus and productivity in non- screen activities
- **Rules:**
  - ○ No devices in the dining room during meals
  - ○ Bedrooms are screen-free zones
  - ○ Use storage bins to keep devices out of designated areas
- **Activities:**
  - ○ Play board games or puzzles in the dining room
  - ○ Read books or engage in creative hobbies in the living room
  - ○ Share daily highlights and engage in family conversations

Creating and maintaining screen-free zones can help build a healthier, more connected family environment. These zones offer a much-needed break from the digital world, allowing everyone to engage more deeply with each other and the activities they enjoy.

Implementing a Gradual Reduction Plan.

Imagine pulling a bandage off your child's skin in one swift motion. The immediate reaction is resistance and discomfort. The same thing happens when you try to cut your child's screen time all at once. Sudden changes can lead to resistance and even withdrawal symptoms, like irritability and increased anxiety. That's why it's important to reduce screen time gradually. By slowly decreasing the time your child spends on their devices, you ease the transition and reduce pushback. This approach makes the change more sustainable, helping your child adjust to a new routine without feeling overwhelmed.

Creating a screen time reduction plan takes some careful thought and planning. Pay attention to how much they spend on different devices and what activities they do. This will help you spot where to reduce their screen time. Next, set realistic and manageable goals. For example, if your child spends five hours a day on screens, try cutting it down by 30 minutes each week. Gradually lowering screen time in small steps avoids a send of loss and helps your child to adjust without feeling too much pressure.

Tracking progress is key to making sure the plan works. There are several methods to help you monitor your child's screen time and make adjustments as needed. Screen time tracking apps are very useful, as they provide detailed reports on how much time is spent on each activity, making it easier to spot patterns and areas for improvement. Another effective method is keeping a screen time journal. Encourage your child to log their daily screen use, including how long they were on and what they did. This not only tracks progress but also helps build self-awareness and accountability.

Getting the whole family involved in the screen time reduction plan can make a big difference. Hold regular family meetings to discuss your goals and track progress. Celebrate milestones and successes together-if your child cuts down their screen time for a week, recognize their effort with a small reward or praise. Encouraging everyone to support each other builds a positive atmosphere where cooperation and commitment thrive. Family member can share their experiences and tips, making the process feel more collaborative and less overwhelming for everyone.

Consider making a visual progress chart to keep the process fun and engaging. Put the chart in a common area, like the kitchen or living room, where everyone can easily see it. Mark each successful day or week with a sticker or a checkmark.

This visual remind can be highly motivating for children, as it gives them a clear of accomplishment. Plus, it serves as a daily reminder of the family's commitment to reducing screen time and creating a healthier balance.

Involving the whole family also means leading an example. Children are more likely to follow the plan if their parents and siblings actively participate. If you're asking your child to cut down on screen time, be ready to do the same. Show them that you prioritize face-to-face interactions and non-screen activities. Plan family outings, game nights, or cooking sessions that encourage everyone to step away from their devices and spend quality time together. This not only reinforces the plan but also strengthens family bonds.

Implementing a gradual reduction plan offers a supportive and structured way to manage screen time. This method reduces resistance, ensures long-lasting changes, and promotes a collaborative family atmosphere. The result is less screen time, more meaningful interactions, improved focus, and a healthier lifestyle for your child.

Engaging Alternatives: Screen-Free Activities

Imagine a rainy afternoon, and your child is feeling restless, about to grab their tablet out of boredom. This is a perfect moment to introduce screen-free activities! These fun alternatives keep children busy and entertained without using digital devices. Plus, they help children develop new skills and interests while sparking creativity, curiosity, and a sense of accomplishment. Whether it's building a model airplane or learning to play an instrument, kids not only pick up a new hobby but also gain patience, problem-solving skills, and a confidence boost.

There are so many screen-free activities to suit different ages and interests! Outdoor games and sports are a great way to keep kids active. Whether it's playing soccer, riding bikes around the neighborhood, or a simple game of tag, these activities provide exercise and a chance to spend time with friends. For kids who love being creative, arts and crafts offer endless fun. Painting, drawing, or making jewelry keeps children busy and lets them express their creativity. Board games and puzzles are also fantastic choices. They promote critical thinking, teamwork, and quality family time. Games like chess, Scrabble, or jigsaw puzzles can be both fun and educational.

Reading and storytelling sessions are a great way to take children on exciting journeys, fueling their imagination while building their language skills. Pick books that match their age and interests, and make reading a fun, shared experience by taking turns reading aloud. This not only expands their vocabulary but also strengthens the parent-child bond. Storytelling can be just as engaging. Encourage your child to invent their own stories and share them with the family. This boosts their creativity, improves their storytelling abilities, and helps build confidence in speaking in front of others.

Incorporating educational activities into your child's routine can make screen-free time both fun and informative. Hands- on learning through science experiments and DIY projects is a great option. Simple experiments like making a baking soda volcano or growing crystals can teach scientific principles in an exciting way. Educational board games and puzzles like "The Game of Life" or "Scrambled States of America" combine fun with learning, helping reinforce concepts like geography, math, and strategy. Reading books on different topics, from history to space exploration, can also expand their knowledge and spark their curiosity.

Try to make screen-free activities a regular habit by integrating them into daily routines. Start by scheduling specific times each day for these activities. For example, you could set aside an hour for outdoor play or arts and crafts after school. Creating a rotating activity calendar can add variety and keep things fresh. Plan different activities for each day of the week, like "Science Experiment Sunday" or "Mystery Book Monday." This way, kids will always have something fun and different to look forward to, making screen-free time a regular and exciting part of their day.

Encouraging children to suggest and plan activities can boost their engagement and excitement. Ask for their ideas and involve them in the planning process. This gives them a sense of ownership and responsibility, making them more eager to participate. For example, if your child loves animals, you could plan a trip to the local zoo or organize a nature scavenger hunt. If they enjoy cooking, spend a Saturday afternoon baking cookies or preparing a family meal together.

Screen-free activities not only reduce reliance on digital devices but also help develop important skills and interests. By offering a variety of activities, adding educational value, and making them part of your daily routine, you can create a balanced and enriching environment for your child.

Setting Clear and Consistent Screen Time Rules

You may often find yourself in a tug-of-war with your child over screen time. One of the best ways to manage this is by setting clear and consistent screen time rules. These rules create structure and predictability, which are important for children. When they know what to expect, it reduces the chances of conflicts and power struggles. For example, if your child knows they can have one hour of screen time after finishing their homework and chores, it helps them manage their expectations and reduces arguments about when and how long they can use their devices.

Setting effective rules involves choosing age-appropriate limits. For younger children, this might mean no more than one hour a day, while older children and teens might be allowed up to two hours, excluding educational purposes. It's also helpful to set specific times and places for screen use. For example, screens could be used only in common areas like the living room and only after school and before dinner. It's just as important to establish clear consequences for breaking the rules, such as losing screen time for a day. This ensures that children understand both the importance of following the rules and the consequences of not doing so.

When explaining these rules, use simple, age-appropriate language. For younger children, you could say, "Screens are for after dinner," while older children might appreciate a more detailed explanation. Involving your child in the process of setting rules can also make them more likely to follow them. When they feel involved, they tend to take more responsibility. Explaining why the rules exist, like balancing screen time with homework, physical activity, and family time, helps them understand the purpose behind the rules, making them less likely to resist.

Enforcing and reviewing these rules is an ongoing process. You can track your child's screen time using apps or by simply keeping an eye on their habits. Family meetings to discuss how the rules are working and any necessary changes help keep them relevant. Encourage open discussions, and listen to your child's feedback. Positive reinforcement, such as praise or small rewards for following the rules, can also motivate your child. This helps make the rules feel like a team effort rather than restrictions, encouraging better cooperation.

A fun way to track screen time and make the process more engaging is by creating a visual chart that outlines the rules and tracks progress. Place the chart in a common area where everyone can see it. Each day your child follows the rules, mark it with a sticker or checkmark. This visual tool not only helps keep track of progress but also serves as a constant reminder of the agreed-upon rules. Involving younger children in this process can be interactive and make them feel more invested.

By setting clear and consistent screen time rules, you create a structured environment where children understand their screen use boundaries. This approach reduces conflicts, encourages responsible behavior, and supports a more balanced lifestyle. The key is communicating clearly, involving your children in setting the rules, and consistently enforcing them with positive reinforcement. This strategy not only helps manage screen time but also fosters responsibility and cooperation, leading to a more harmonious home environment.

Leveraging Technology: Parental Control Tools

As a parent, you may often feel like you're constantly competing with screens for your child's attention. One helpful solution is using parental control tools. These tools allow you to manage screen time effectively by monitoring usage, blocking inappropriate content, and setting time limits and schedules. Think of them as a digital gatekeeper, giving you control over what your child can access and for how long. Imagine knowing exactly how much time your child spends on each app and being able to set restrictions that match your family's needs. This control can bring a sense of peace and order to your home.

Choosing the right parental control tools is key to their success. Start by considering tools that are compatible with all your child's devices, whether it's an iPhone, Android tablet, or laptop. The tool should work seamlessly across platforms. Ease of use is also crucial—look for tools with simple interfaces that make setup and management easy and quick.

Additionally, think about the features you need. Some tools offer basic functions like time limits and monitoring, while others provide advanced options like content filtering, location tracking, and detailed usage reports. Choose a tool that fits your family's needs without being overly complicated.

Once you've chosen a tool, implementing it is straightforward. Install the software on your child's devices and configure the settings to your preferences. This may include setting time limits, blocking specific websites, or scheduling device use during certain hours. It's important to regularly review and adjust these settings as your child grows and their needs change. For example, you may allow more screen time during school holidays or restrict certain apps during exam periods.

Balancing control and trust is essential when using these tools. While they help manage screen time, they shouldn't replace open communication and trust with your child. Explain why you've put parental controls in place—so they can use technology responsibly and stay safe. Encourage open conversations about screen usage and listen to their thoughts and concerns. This builds mutual respect and cooperation. As your child demonstrates responsible behavior, you can gradually loosen the controls, allowing more freedom. Rewarding good behavior helps them develop self-regulation skills, fostering both independence and trust.

For example, one family I know used Google's Family Link to manage their child's screen time. They started with strict limits but gradually increased the allowed screen time as their child showed responsible behavior. The children appreciated the trust and responsibility they were given, which motivated them to follow the rules. Another family used Apple's Screen Time to set app limits and downtime schedules. They explained to their teenagers that the controls weren't meant to punish but to help maintain a balanced lifestyle, ensuring time for family, homework, and outdoor activities. The teens respected the rules because they understood the reasoning and felt involved in the process.

Incorporating parental control tools into your family's routine can greatly help manage screen time. These tools provide a practical solution for monitoring and limiting screen usage, blocking inappropriate content, and setting schedules. By selecting the right tools, implementing them thoughtfully, and balancing control with trust, you can create a safer, more balanced digital environment for your children.

Promoting Outdoor Play and Physical Activities

Outdoor play offers numerous benefits that are essential for your child's health and development. When children engage in outdoor physical activities like running, jumping, and climbing, they improve their fitness, motor skills, strength, coordination, and agility. But the benefits don't stop at the physical level—outdoor play also nurtures creativity and problem-solving skills. Children naturally invent games, explore their surroundings, and use their imagination to create new scenarios, all of which contribute to cognitive development and critical thinking.

Being outdoors also positively impacts mental health and emotional well-being. Fresh air and natural light help reduce stress, boost mood, and create a sense of calm—important benefits for children who spend much of their time on screens.

Encouraging more outdoor play can be challenging, but it's definitely achievable. One effective approach is to plan regular family outings. These don't need to be elaborate; a simple visit to a park, a hike on a nearby trail, or a beach day can offer great opportunities for outdoor fun. Creating an inviting outdoor space at home can also motivate children to play outside more often. Setting up a sandbox, swing set, or small garden where they can dig and plant can make outdoor time more appealing. Introducing new activities and sports, like soccer or a casual game of catch, can keep them engaged and excited about being outside.

Balancing indoor and outdoor activities is key to maintaining a healthy lifestyle. You can set daily or weekly outdoor play goals to make outdoor time part of your routine. For example, aim for at least one hour of outdoor play each day or plan more extensive activities on weekends. Limiting screen time can also encourage more outdoor activity, as children are more likely to seek other forms of entertainment when screens are restricted. This balance allows them to enjoy indoor comforts while also reaping the benefits of outdoor experiences.

Parental involvement is crucial in promoting outdoor play. Children are more likely to participate in activities when their parents are actively involved. Joining your child in outdoor games, sports, or family challenges like a scavenger hunt or bike ride can add excitement and provide bonding time. Modeling an active lifestyle and enthusiasm for outdoor play also sets a positive example, showing children the joy and importance of staying active outdoors.

One family I know transformed their backyard into an adventure zone, complete with a treehouse, zip line, and a small garden where the kids could grow vegetables. This became the favorite place for after-school play and weekend fun. Not only did the children get plenty of exercise, but they also learned valuable lessons about nature and responsibility. Another family organized weekly "nature days" to explore different parks and reserves. Each outing featured a new activity—bird watching, rock climbing, or even a simple picnic by a lake. These experiences enriched their children's lives in ways screen time never could.

Promoting outdoor play involves creating an environment that supports and encourages time outside. By planning regular outings, setting up inviting play spaces, balancing indoor and outdoor activities, and actively participating in them, you can nurture your child's love for the outdoors. This love not only boosts physical health but also enhances creativity, emotional well-being, and overall quality of life. As these strategies become part of your routine, you'll see the benefits extend beyond your children, enriching family life as a whole.

Balancing screen time with outdoor play and physical activities leads to a healthier, more engaging lifestyle for children. Being proactive and involved helps set the stage for a well-rounded childhood that nurtures both body and mind. This approach also lays the groundwork for lifelong habits that prioritize health, creativity, and emotional well-being. Next, we'll explore how to foster healthy digital habits, ensuring that technology enhances rather than hinders your child's development.

CHAPTER 4

Fostering Healthy Digital Habits

One afternoon, I watched a family in the park. The parents were playing catch with their young children, their laughter echoing through the air. Nearby, another child sat alone on a bench, completely absorbed in a tablet. The contrast was striking. While technology certainly has its place, it often pulls us away from the people and experiences right in front of us. This chapter is about finding that balance and helping our children learn to use technology mindfully and with intention.

Teaching Mindful Tech Use.

Understanding mindful technology use is essential in today's digital world. It means being intentional with the time spent on devices and knowing the difference between productive and mindless screen time. Mindful tech use involves setting clear goals for each session, whether it's for completing homework, learning a new skill, or simply relaxing with a movie. The key is to use technology as a tool, not a crutch.

One common issue is mindless scrolling, which can easily eat up hours without providing any real benefit. Teaching children to recognize when they're engaging in this behavior and to redirect their focus toward more purposeful activities is crucial. By becoming aware of how they spend their time online, children can make more conscious choices that support their well-being and development.

There are practical ways to help children develop mindful tech habits. Setting specific goals for each tech session creates a sense of purpose. For instance, if your child uses a tablet for educational games, encourage them to aim for completing a certain number of levels or mastering a new concept. This keeps their screen time focused and productive. Regular breaks are also essential. Encourage your child to pause every 20-30 minutes to check in with how they're feeling, helping to reduce eye strain and avoid digital fatigue.

As parents, modeling mindful tech use is one of the most powerful ways to teach these habits. Show your children focused, purposeful screen use by scheduling times to check emails or scroll through social media and sticking to that schedule. Practicing regular digital detoxes, where the whole family spends a day or weekend without screens, can demonstrate that life is enjoyable without constant digital interruptions. These detoxes can even become family traditions, allowing for more time together doing activities like hiking, cooking, or playing games.

Incorporating mindfulness practices into daily routines can complement mindful tech use. Apps offering guided mindfulness exercises are a great tool for both parents and children, providing short sessions that teach relaxation techniques like breathing and meditation. These exercises can be done during tech breaks or at the beginning or end of the day to create a calm, focused mindset. Another useful practice is encouraging children to journal about their digital experiences. Provide them with a notebook and ask them to write about what they did online, how it made them feel, and what they learned. This reflection helps them become more aware of their digital habits and their impact.

Interactive Element: Mindful Tech Use Checklist

Creating a checklist can be a great way to help your child practice mindful technology use. Place it near their study area or wherever they spend time on their devices.

1. **Set a Purpose**: What is the goal for this tech session? (e.g., complete homework, learn a new skill)

2. **Time Limit**: How long will you use the device? Set a timer.

3. **Regular Breaks**: Take a 5-minute break every 20 minutes.

4. **Reflect**: After the session, write down what you did and how it made you feel.

By following this checklist, your child can develop the habit of mindful screen use, making their time online more intentional and beneficial. Encouraging these practices helps foster a balanced approach to technology, ensuring that it enhances rather than detracts from their overall well-being. This balanced mindset will empower them to use technology as a tool for learning, creativity, and relaxation while maintaining a healthy, well-rounded lifestyle.

Encouraging Screen Breaks and Tech Timeouts

It's easy to lose track of time when immersed in a screen, whether it's a computer, tablet, or smartphone. However, prolonged screen time can lead to eye strain, fatigue, and even headaches. The constant focus on a screen can overwork the eyes, causing discomfort and making it hard to concentrate on other tasks. Regular breaks are crucial for reducing eye strain and preventing digital overload. When children take breaks, their eyes get the rest they need, lowering the risk of long-term damage. Additionally, breaks help prevent mental fatigue, as children, like adults, can experience burnout from too much screen time, which can lead to irritability and decreased productivity.

Setting up tech timeouts within daily routines can be an effective way to manage screen time. One popular method is the 20-20-20 rule for eye health. This rule suggests that for every 20 minutes spent on a screen, you should take a 20- second break and look at something 20 feet away. This simple practice helps alleviate eye strain and keeps vision sharp. Another strategy is scheduling hourly breaks during longer screen sessions. Encourage your child to step away from their device for at least five minutes every hour. These breaks can be used to stretch, move around, or simply rest their eyes, creating a healthier balance between screen time and other activities. This balance makes it easier for children to maintain focus and overall well-being.

Several tools and methods can help remind children to take these essential breaks. Break reminder apps are a practical solution. These apps can be set to alert your child at regular intervals, prompting them to step away from their screen. Alternatively, physical timers or alarms can serve the same purpose. Setting a kitchen timer or an alarm on a non-digital clock can signal it's time for a break. You could also establish a fun family "tech timeout" signal, such as a special gesture or phrase, to remind everyone to take a break from their screens in an engaging way.

Making these breaks enjoyable and effective is key. Simple activities like stretching exercises or yoga poses can help relieve the physical tension caused by sitting for too long, improving flexibility and circulation. Quick outdoor activities, like jumping jacks or a short walk, can provide a boost of energy and a refreshing change of scenery. Even a few minutes outside can clear the mind. Alternatively, engaging in creative tasks like drawing, playing an instrument, or doodling offers a mental break and stimulates creativity. These activities give your child's brain the opportunity to reset and recharge, making them feel more refreshed and ready to focus again.

Interactive Element: Tech Timeout Activity Ideas

Here's a list of activities your child can choose from during tech timeouts. You can place it in a visible spot near their study area or on the refrigerator.

1. **Stretching Exercises**: Try a few yoga poses or simple stretches.

2. **Quick Outdoor Activities**: Take a five-minute walk or do some jumping jacks.

3. **Creative Tasks**: Draw a picture, play a musical instrument, or write a short story.

4. **Relaxation**: Practice deep breathing exercises or listen to a calming song.

By incorporating these screen breaks and tech timeouts into daily routines, you can help your child develop healthier screen habits. These breaks not only reduce the physical and mental strain of prolonged screen use but also offer chances to engage in different activities that support overall well-being. As you integrate these practices, you'll notice your child becoming more balanced, focused, and happier, both during their screen time and in their offline activities.

Understanding and Managing Digital Footprints

When your child posts a photo on social media or comments on a friend's post, they create a digital footprint. This footprint includes the data trails left behind from all online activities, such as social media posts, online searches, and even content that others share about them. These digital traces are more permanent than they might seem. Once something is posted online, it can be very difficult to remove entirely. This permanence can have long-term implications for privacy, security, and even future opportunities. Colleges and employers often review an individual's online presence when making admissions or hiring decisions. Helping your child understand the significance of their digital footprint is essential for guiding them toward responsible online behavior.

Educating children about managing their digital footprints begins with explaining the permanence of online posts. Make sure they understand that once something is shared, it can be copied, shared, and archived, making it almost impossible to erase completely. This means that posts made impulsively or in the heat of the moment can have long-lasting effects. Encourage your child to think before they post, considering how their words and images might be perceived by others. Teaching them about responsible sharing and how to use privacy settings is another important step. Show them how to adjust privacy settings on social media platforms so they can control who sees their posts, and explain why sharing personal information should be limited to trusted friends and family.

There are practical steps you can take to help your child manage their digital footprint. Encourage them to regularly review and clean up their social media profiles. Periodically going through old posts and removing content that no longer reflects their values or could be misunderstood is a good habit. Using privacy settings wisely is also key. Teach them how to customize privacy options so that only trusted individuals can access their posts and personal information. This helps protect their privacy and ensures their online presence remains positive. Additionally, remind them to be selective about who they accept as friends or followers, connecting only with people they know and trust.

Parental involvement is vital in helping children understand and manage their online presence. Regularly monitor their online activities and guide them toward appropriate behavior by discussing what they do online. Talk about the potential consequences of oversharing or posting inappropriate content. Share real-life examples of individuals who have faced negative consequences for their online behavior to emphasize the importance of responsible digital conduct. Keep the lines of communication open so that your child feels comfortable discussing their online experiences and any concerns they might have.

Interactive Element: Digital Footprint Reflection Prompts

Reflecting on their online behavior can help your child become more mindful of their digital footprint. Here are some prompts to help start a conversation or journaling activity:

1. **What types of information do you share online? Why do you choose to share this information?**

2. **Have you ever posted something online that you later regretted? What did you learn from that experience?**

3. **How do you think your online posts might be interpreted by someone who doesn't know you well?**

4. **What steps can you take to ensure your online presence reflects who you want to be?**

By helping your child understand and manage their digital footprints, you guide them toward a safer and more positive online experience. This awareness not only protects their privacy and reputation but also fosters responsible and thoughtful online behavior. As these practices become part of your family's routine, you'll notice your child becoming more mindful of their digital presence, leading to a healthier, more secure, and conscientious approach to their online life.

Promoting Cyber Hygiene

Cyber hygiene has become a cornerstone of online safety in today's interconnected world. Cyber hygiene refers to the practices and steps individuals take to maintain the health of their digital systems and protect personal information from cyber threats. For children, understanding and practicing good cyber hygiene is crucial to ensure their online activities are safe and secure, shielding them from potential dangers such as identity theft, cyberbullying, and exposure to inappropriate content. As parents, fostering these habits early on can help your children navigate the digital world more safely and responsibly.

Protecting personal information is a key aspect of cyber hygiene. Children often share details online without fully grasping the risks involved. Teach your child the importance of keeping personal information private, including their full name, address, phone number, and school details. Explain that sharing this information can make them vulnerable to cyber threats. Encourage them to be cautious about what they post and with whom they share it, emphasizing that not everyone online has good intentions.

Basic cyber hygiene practices can significantly improve your child's online safety. One of the most effective steps is using unique, strong passwords for different accounts. A strong password usually includes a mix of letters, numbers, and special characters, making it harder for hackers to guess. Encourage your child to avoid using easily guessable information like their name or birthdate. Another important practice is avoiding suspicious links and downloads. Teach your child to be wary of clicking on links in unsolicited emails or pop-up ads, as these may lead to malicious websites or download harmful malware. Explain that downloading files from unknown sources can infect their devices with viruses or spyware, potentially compromising their personal information.

Advanced cyber safety measures offer even more protection. Enabling two-factor authentication (2FA) adds an extra layer of security to online accounts. With 2FA, even if someone gets access to your child's password, they will need a second verification form, like a code sent to their phone, to gain access to the account. Regularly updating software and security patches is another crucial measure. These updates often fix security vulnerabilities that cybercriminals could exploit. Make it a habit to check for and install updates promptly, ensuring your child's devices are protected against the latest threats.

As parents, your role in promoting and ensuring cyber hygiene is essential. Setting up and monitoring parental controls can help manage your child's online activities. These controls can restrict access to inappropriate content, set time limits on device usage, and monitor online interactions. It's also important to educate your children about phishing and other online scams. Phishing scams often come in the form of emails or messages that look legitimate but are designed to steal personal information. Teach your child to recognize red flags, such as misspelled URLs, unsolicited requests for personal information, or offers that seem too good to be true.

By instilling these cyber hygiene habits, you can empower your children to use the internet safely and responsibly, reducing the risks associated with the digital world.

Interactive Element: Cyber Hygiene Checklist

A checklist can help your child remember and practice good cyber hygiene habits. Place it near their computer or study area as a constant reminder.

1. **Use Strong, Unique Passwords**: Include letters, numbers, and special characters.

2. **Avoid Suspicious Links**: Don't click on links in unsolicited emails or pop-ups.

3. **Enable Two-Factor Authentication**: Add an extra layer of security to accounts.

4. **Update Software Regularly**: Install updates and security patches promptly.

5. **Protect Personal Information**: Keep details like full name, address, and phone number private.

Integrating these practices into your family's routine can help your child develop strong cyber hygiene habits. These habits not only protect their personal information and online activities but also foster a sense of responsibility and awareness about the digital world. By guiding your child through these practices, they'll gain the confidence and skills to navigate online spaces safely and securely, ready to handle the challenges and opportunities of being digitally connected. This foundation ensures they are better equipped to manage their digital presence responsibly and stay safe in an increasingly connected world.

Incorporating Educational Screen Time Wisely

When considering screen time, not all screen use is created equal. Differentiating between educational and non- educational screen time is crucial for fostering a balanced digital environment for your children. Educational screen time involves engaging with apps, programs, and content that promote learning and development. These include interactive math games, science simulations, and language learning apps. Identifying quality educational content requires a discerning eye. Look for age-appropriate and curriculum-aligned programs, ensuring they complement what your child is learning in school. Reviews and recommendations from trusted sources such as educators or educational websites can guide you in selecting the best tools. Interactive and engaging learning platforms, which encourage active participation rather than passive consumption, are particularly beneficial. They can turn screen time into a productive and enjoyable learning experience.

Balancing educational content with entertainment is another critical aspect. While it's essential to incorporate learning tools, children also need downtime to enjoy themselves simply. The key is creating a balanced schedule with educational and recreational screen time. This approach ensures that your child benefits from the enriching aspects of technology without feeling deprived of fun. For instance, you might set aside specific time for weekday educational apps and allow more entertainment-focused screen time on weekends. This balance helps maintain a positive attitude towards screen use while promoting overall development.

Selecting high-quality educational content involves a few key steps. First, ensure the resources are age-appropriate, matching your child's cognitive and emotional maturity. Curriculum-aligned resources are also valuable as they reinforce what your child is learning in school. This alignment can make learning more cohesive and relevant. Reviews and recommendations from trusted sources can provide insights into various apps and programs' effectiveness and engagement levels. Look for feedback from educators, parents, and educational organizations to make informed choices. Interactive and engaging learning platforms are particularly effective as they encourage active participation and critical thinking. These platforms often include features like quizzes, interactive lessons, and progress tracking, which can make learning more dynamic and personalized.

Integrating educational screen time into daily and weekly routines can be seamless with some planning. Setting specific times for educational apps or programs helps create a structured environment. For instance, you might designate a half-hour after school for educational apps before transitioning to other activities. Combining screen learning with hands-on activities can also enhance the learning experience. If your child uses an app to learn about plant biology, follow it up with a hands-on activity like planting seeds or visiting a botanical garden. This approach reinforces what they've learned and makes the information more tangible and memorable.

Reviewing and reflecting on educational content is essential for ensuring meaningful and effective learning. After each session, take a few minutes to discuss what your child learned. Ask them to explain new concepts in their own words and share their thoughts. This not only reinforces the material but also promotes critical thinking and communication skills. Encourage your child to ask questions and express their curiosity, as this can lead to a deeper understanding and more engagement with the subject. Consider keeping a learning journal where your child can jot down key takeaways and reflections after each session. This journal can serve as a valuable tool for tracking progress, identifying areas of interest, and pinpointing any challenges.

Incorporating educational screen time involves selecting high-quality content, balancing it with entertainment, and making it a part of structured routines. Reviewing and reflecting on the content ensures that your child's screen time is both enriching and enjoyable. This balanced approach fosters a lifelong love of learning and helps develop a healthy, intentional relationship with technology.

Balancing Online and Offline Social Interactions

The digital age has brought both benefits and drawbacks to children's social interactions. On one hand, online platforms enable children to maintain connections with distant friends and family members, helping to strengthen relationships that might otherwise fade due to distance. For example, video calls with grandparents or messaging a friend who moved away can keep these bonds alive. However, the online world also has its pitfalls. Cyberbullying is an ever-present threat, where children may face harassment and emotional distress from peers. Moreover, social comparison on platforms like Instagram and Snapchat can lead to feelings of inadequacy and low self-esteem, as children often compare their lives to the curated, often unrealistic portrayals they see online.

To guide your child toward healthy online interactions, it's important to set respectful communication guidelines. Teach them the value of kindness and empathy in their online exchanges. Explain that the anonymity of the internet doesn't excuse hurtful behavior and that their words can have a lasting impact. Monitoring online activities without being overly intrusive also plays a critical role. By keeping an eye on their digital interactions, you can catch any signs of cyberbullying or inappropriate behavior early. If you see anything concerning, address it calmly and supportively, offering guidance on how to handle the situation.

Encouraging offline social skills is equally important in today's tech-driven world. Organizing playdates and group activities provides opportunities for face-to-face interactions, which help children develop social skills like sharing, cooperation, and conflict resolution. Participation in clubs, sports, and community events offers additional avenues for social engagement. Whether it's joining a soccer team, participating in a drama club, or attending community service events, these activities help children build friendships and develop a sense of belonging. They also provide a healthy contrast to the often solitary nature of online interactions.

Maintaining a balance between screen time and face-to-face interactions requires thoughtful planning and consistency.

Setting limits on social media and messaging app usage helps ensure that online interactions don't overshadow real-world relationships. Designating specific times for online activities and enforcing rules like putting away devices during family meals and outings can help. Prioritizing in-person time with family and friends over online interactions fosters stronger, more meaningful relationships. Encouraging activities that bring the family together—like game nights, outdoor adventures, or shared meals without screens—teaches children the value of real-world connections.

One family found success by implementing a "technology-free Sunday." Every Sunday, they would disconnect from their devices and spend the day together doing activities such as hiking, playing board games, and trying out new recipes. This practice strengthened their family bonds and taught the children the joy of offline interactions. Another family encouraged their children to join local sports teams and participate in neighborhood events. This involvement helped the children build friendships and develop social skills beyond the digital world.

Balancing online and offline social interactions is about creating a harmonious blend of digital and real-world experiences. By setting guidelines for respectful online communication, monitoring activities, encouraging offline interactions, and prioritizing face-to-face time, you can help your child navigate the complexities of social life in the digital age. These efforts enhance their social skills and improve their overall well-being and development.

This chapter explores various strategies for fostering healthy digital habits, from mindful tech use and screen breaks to understanding digital footprints and promoting cyber hygiene.

These practices play a crucial role in helping children navigate the digital world safely and responsibly. As we move forward, we'll delve into the next chapter, discussing strengthening family bonds through shared activities and meaningful interactions.

CHAPTER 5

Strengthening Family Bonds

One chilly winter evening, I visited a friend's home and was greeted by a scene that felt both nostalgic and heartwarming. The whole family was gathered around the dining table, deeply involved in a board game. Laughter filled the air as they debated the rules and celebrated small victories. This simple yet meaningful activity highlighted the power of shared experiences. In today's fast-paced, screen-dominated world, family game nights offer a much-needed break, creating opportunities to deepen connections and build joyful memories that last a lifetime.

Family Game Nights: Fun Without Screens

The Benefits of Family Game Nights

Family game nights are more than just fun—they are a powerful tool for building communication and strengthening bonds. When everyone gathers to play, it creates an environment of teamwork and cooperation. Many games require players to work together to solve problems or achieve common goals, fostering a sense of unity and mutual support. This cooperation extends beyond the game, teaching valuable skills that can be applied to daily life.

In addition to promoting teamwork, family game nights offer a fun and engaging way to spend time together. In an era where screens often dominate our attention, these evenings provide a much-needed, enjoyable screen-free alternative. They create opportunities for face-to-face interactions, shared laughter, and the creation of lasting memories. Moreover, replacing screen time with interactive play helps reduce overall time spent on devices, promoting healthier habits and stronger family connections. Through these shared experiences, family game nights help build relationships and create a sense of togetherness that is both enjoyable and enriching.

Choosing the Right Games

Selecting suitable games is crucial for ensuring everyone has a great time during family game nights. It's important to choose games that cater to all age groups involved, ensuring that both young children and adults can enjoy the experience together. Board games and card games are ideal options for this purpose. Look for games that promote teamwork and problem-solving, as these enhance the collaborative spirit of the evening. For instance, games like "Settlers of Catan" require strategic thinking and teamwork, making them perfect for older children and adults. For a simpler option, "Uno" is a classic card game that younger children can grasp easily but remains engaging for older players as well.

Interactive games that encourage movement, such as "Twister," can bring an element of physical activity and fun to the evening. These games keep everyone actively engaged and promote physical coordination, adding an extra layer of excitement to family game night. By choosing games that match the ages and interests of your family members, you can create a lively and inclusive atmosphere that everyone will enjoy, building both memories and stronger bonds.

Making It a Tradition

Establishing family game nights as a regular tradition creates a sense of anticipation and consistency that everyone can look forward to. Start by choosing a specific day and time for the event each week, whether it's Friday evenings or Sunday afternoons. Having a fixed schedule allows everyone to plan around it and build excitement for the activity. Rotating game choices each week keeps things fresh and engaging. Allow a different family member to pick the game, ensuring variety and personal involvement. This rotation not only prevents monotony but also allows everyone to introduce their favorite games or try something new together.

Creating a fun atmosphere is key to making these nights memorable. Special snacks and treats can elevate the experience, turning it into a mini celebration. Prepare popcorn, homemade cookies, or a favorite family recipe to enjoy during the game. You can also introduce themed game nights to add an extra layer of excitement. For example, a pirate-themed night could include eye patches and pirate lingo, while a pajama party night could feature cozy blankets and hot chocolate.

Encouraging friendly competition and positive reinforcement is important. Celebrate small victories and good sportsmanship with praise and rewards, creating a positive and supportive environment. By making family game nights fun, inclusive, and consistent, you'll create lasting memories and a tradition that strengthens family bonds.

Interactive Element: Family Game Night Planner

1. **Choose a Fixed Day and Time**: Decide on a day and time each week for game night.

2. **Rotate Game Choices**: Assign each family member a turn to pick the game.

3. **Prepare Special Snacks**: Plan and prepare snacks to enjoy during the game.

4. **Create Themes**: Introduce fun themes to make each game night unique.

Incorporating these elements can transform family game nights into a cherished tradition, promoting stronger family bonds and creating joyful, screen-free memories. As you continue to explore ways to strengthen your family connections, remember that the goal is to reduce screen time and replace it with meaningful, engaging activities that bring you closer together.

Device-Free Dinners: Reclaiming Meal Times

Imagine sitting down for dinner with your family, and instead of the usual silent scrolling, the room is filled with laughter and lively conversation. This simple shift can make a world of difference. Device-free dinners are essential for fostering family bonding and communication. When everyone puts their screens away, it opens the door for meaningful face-to- face conversations. These moments are invaluable, allowing family members to connect, share stories, and better understand each other's experiences.

Additionally, focusing on the meal encourages mindful eating, which benefits digestion. Without the distraction of screens, everyone is more aware of what they're eating and how much, leading to healthier habits. Reducing distractions also enhances focus on family interactions, making each meal a time to reconnect and enjoy each other's company.

Establishing device-free dinner rules can be simple with a few key steps. Start by designating a spot for storing devices during meals— perhaps a basket or drawer where everyone places their phones and tablets before sitting down. It's important to explain the reasons behind this rule, ensuring everyone understands that it's about improving family communication and creating a more enjoyable dining experience. As parents, leading by example is crucial. If you commit to device-free dinners, your children are more likely to follow suit. Consistency is key—over time, this practice will become a natural part of your family routine.

To keep conversations flowing during device-free dinners, having a few engaging conversation starters can be incredibly helpful. Encourage each person to share the best and worst parts of their day. This not only provides insight into each other's lives but also sparks meaningful discussions. Discussing interesting news or asking open-ended questions, like "What made you laugh today?" or "If you could travel anywhere, where would you go?" can invite thoughtful responses and ensure everyone feels involved. The goal is to create a comfortable space where everyone feels heard and connected.

Making meals special can elevate the experience and make family members look forward to dinner time. Preparing favorite family recipes together can be a fun, bonding activity. Get everyone involved in the process—from choosing the menu to cooking and setting the table. This shared effort adds a personal touch and makes the meal feel even more meaningful. Setting the table with simple decorations, like a tablecloth, candles, or flowers, can create a warm and inviting atmosphere. Occasionally, themed dinners can bring an extra element of fun. Whether it's an Italian night with pasta and cannoli or a taco Tuesday with a build-your-own taco bar, themed meals add excitement and make the experience more memorable.

Interactive Element: Conversation Starters List

1. **Best and Worst Parts of the Day**: Share one highlight and challenge from your day.

2. **Exciting News**: Discuss a recent news story that caught your attention.

3. **Open-Ended Questions:**

   ○ What made you laugh today?

   ○ If you could travel anywhere, where would you go?

   ○ What is something new you learned this week?

Device-free dinners are more than just a break from screens— they are a chance to foster deeper connections, promote healthy eating habits, and create a more engaging and enjoyable dining experience for the entire family. By setting clear rules, leading by example, and making mealtimes special, you can reclaim dinner time as a cherished family tradition. These moments not only strengthen family bonds but also provide a space for meaningful conversations, mindfulness, and shared joy.

Collaborative Projects and Crafts

Imagine a rainy Saturday afternoon transformed into a time of connection and creativity through a family project that keeps everyone engaged. Collaborative projects are an excellent way to unite your family, encouraging teamwork, problem-solving, and shared accomplishment. As you and your children work together, from brainstorming ideas to completing the project, you cultivate a sense of pride and cooperation. These hands-on activities also provide a rewarding, screen-free alternative, reducing time spent on devices and promoting meaningful engagement.

There are countless collaborative projects to suit different interests and age groups. DIY home improvement projects, such as building a birdhouse, can be both practical and fun, with each family member contributing their skills and ideas. Art and craft projects, like painting or scrapbooking, let creativity flow while creating lasting memories. Gardening is another excellent option, teaching patience and responsibility as you plant a garden together that will beautify your home. Each project offers a unique opportunity to bond and create something meaningful as a family.

To make collaborative projects a regular part of your routine, it's important to organize project time. Start by setting aside regular time slots, like a specific day each week or a few hours on the weekend, for project work. Breaking projects into manageable steps helps keep them enjoyable rather than overwhelming. Encouraging everyone to contribute their ideas and skills fosters a sense of inclusion and excitement. For instance, if you're building a birdhouse, one person might measure and cut the wood, another could paint it, and someone else could assemble the pieces. This approach ensures that everyone feels valued and involved.

Celebrating completed projects is an essential part of the process, reinforcing the sense of accomplishment and pride in your family's work. You could host a "project reveal" party, inviting friends and extended family to admire what you've created together. Additionally, creating a dedicated space in your home to display finished projects—a shelf, a wall, or a corner of the living room—keeps these memories alive. Another idea is to document your efforts in a family journal, with photos, descriptions, and reflections from each family member on what the project meant to them. This journal can serve as a beautiful keepsake of your shared experiences and accomplishments.

Interactive Element: Project Planning Guide

1. **Set Regular Time Slots**: Choose a specific day or time each week for projects.

2. **Break into Manageable Steps**: Divide the project into smaller tasks.

3. **Encourage Contributions**: Let each family member take on a role.

4. **Celebrate Completion**: Host a reveal party or create a display space.

Incorporating collaborative projects into your family's routine offers a rich and rewarding way to spend time together. These activities foster creativity, teamwork, and a sense of pride, while also providing a meaningful alternative to screen time. Through these shared efforts, your family can create lasting memories and build stronger bonds, making each project an opportunity to connect and grow together.

Outdoor Adventures and Nature Walks

The Benefits of Outdoor Activities

Picture a sunny afternoon when the entire family heads to a local park. The benefits of spending time outdoors together are immense. Physical fitness and health top the list, as walking, hiking, or playing outdoor games keeps everyone active, promoting cardiovascular health and building strength. The fresh air and natural light also contribute to overall well- being, helping to reduce the risk of various health issues. Mentally, being outdoors acts as a natural stress reliever. The sights and sounds of nature have a calming effect, reducing stress and improving moods—especially beneficial for children dealing with academic pressures. Emotionally, spending time in nature cultivates a deeper appreciation for the environment, fostering wonder and curiosity about the world around us. This connection to nature can be incredibly grounding, offering a much-needed break from the constant digital stimuli we encounter every day.

Planning Outdoor Adventures

Planning outdoor activities can be a fun and rewarding experience for the whole family. Start by researching local parks and nature reserves—websites and visitor centers often provide maps, trail details, and suggestions for activities. Packing essentials is key to ensuring a successful outing. Be sure to bring water, snacks, and a basic first-aid kit to keep everyone hydrated, nourished, and prepared for minor injuries. When selecting activities, choose ones that cater to all fitness levels in your family. For example, hiking trails with varying difficulty levels can accommodate different abilities. A family picnic is another wonderful way to enjoy a meal together in a natural setting, offering a relaxed and enjoyable experience.

For added excitement, consider organizing a nature scavenger hunt. This can turn your outing into an adventure, encouraging children to explore and learn about the natural world. Activities like these not only keep everyone engaged but also provide opportunities for learning, bonding, and building lasting memories together.

Engaging Activities in Nature

Engaging in interactive activities during your outdoor adventures can make the experience even more enriching. Birdwatching, for instance, is a fascinating activity that can captivate all ages. Bring along a field guide or use a birdwatching app to help identify different species, encouraging patience and keen observation skills. Collecting leaves, rocks, or other natural items for a nature journal is another creative way to engage. Children can document their discoveries by drawing or writing about each item, deepening their appreciation for nature while providing a creative outlet.

Playing outdoor games like Frisbee or Capture the Flag introduces an element of physical activity and fun. These games promote teamwork and cooperation, fostering a sense of unity within the family. Each of these activities not only offers a refreshing break from screens but also promotes physical health and mental well-being, creating shared experiences that are both enjoyable and meaningful.

Making It a Habit

Consider setting a weekly or monthly outdoor adventure day to make outdoor activities a regular part of family life. Consistency builds anticipation and turns these outings into a cherished tradition. Involve your children in the planning process by allowing them to choose the destination or activities for the day. This involvement not only gives them a sense of ownership but also builds excitement around the adventure.

Documenting your adventures with photos and keeping a nature journal can help preserve these special moments. Each entry could include pictures, descriptions, and personal reflections on the day's experiences. This journal serves as a meaningful keepsake of your family's time together, fostering a deeper connection to nature and strengthening family bonds. It also offers a way to reflect on your shared experiences and growth over time.

Interactive Element: Nature Scavenger Hunt List

1. **Birdwatching**: Identify and list five different bird species.

2. **Leaf Collection**: Collect leaves from three different trees and describe their shapes.

3. **Rock Hunt**: Find rocks with unique colors or patterns.

4. **Insect Observation**: Spot and draw two different insects.

Making outdoor activities a regular part of your family routine offers countless benefits. These adventures provide opportunities for exercise, stress relief, and a deeper appreciation for nature. By planning engaging activities and making outdoor time a consistent habit, you can foster stronger family bonds while creating lasting memories that everyone will cherish for years to come.

Storytelling and Reading Together

Imagine the scene: Your family is gathered in the living room, the lights dimmed, and the focus entirely on the book in your hands. The magic of storytelling and reading together lies in its simplicity and profound impact. When you read aloud to your children, you not only enhance their language and literacy skills, but also create a rich bonding experience. The rhythm and cadence of your voice help them grasp vocabulary and sentence structure, laying a solid foundation for their reading and speaking abilities. Beyond these academic benefits, storytelling fosters imagination and creativity. As you weave tales of far-off lands or brave heroes, your children visualize these worlds, stretching their creative muscles. This shared experience becomes a cherished ritual, strengthening emotional bonds as you connect deeply through the story, exchanging thoughts, questions, and emotions along the way.

Choosing the right stories and books is key to maintaining this magical atmosphere. It's important to select age-appropriate and interest-based books that captivate your children's attention. Books with positive messages and diverse characters offer valuable lessons and broaden their understanding of the world. A mix of genres and formats keeps the experience fresh and engaging. Picture books are perfect for younger children, while chapter books can capture the imagination of older kids. Audiobooks can also be a great addition, providing a different sensory experience. Classics like the *Harry Potter* series transport readers to a world of magic and friendship, *Charlotte's Web* teaches lessons about friendship and sacrifice, and *The Lion, the Witch and the Wardrobe* takes you on an adventure through a fantastical land filled with moral dilemmas.

Establishing a regular reading routine can turn storytelling into a beloved family tradition. Set aside a specific time each day or week dedicated to reading together. This consistency helps build anticipation and integrates reading into the rhythm of your family's life. Creating a cozy and inviting reading space enhances the experience—fill it with comfortable seating, soft lighting, and a few stuffed animals or pillows to make it a welcoming retreat. Taking turns reading aloud allows everyone to actively participate. Discussing the story as you go along deepens understanding and engagement. Ask open- ended questions about the characters' motivations or plot twists to spark thoughtful conversations and encourage critical thinking.

Interactive storytelling activities can further enrich the experience, making it more engaging and memorable. Acting out scenes from the stories brings them to life in a fun and dynamic way. Encourage your children to use their imagination to create simple costumes or props. This role- playing not only makes the story more vivid but also helps develop confidence and public speaking skills. Creating illustrations or crafts based on the books is another exciting activity. Let your children draw their favorite scenes or characters, or work together on a craft project inspired by the story. These creative endeavors create a tangible connection to the story, making it more memorable.

Writing and sharing original family stories can be an excellent way to bond and explore creativity. Encourage each family member to contribute a part of the story, building it together chapter by chapter. This collaborative storytelling can lead to delightful surprises and become a unique family narrative that everyone will treasure for years to come.

Incorporating storytelling and reading into your family's routine offers numerous benefits beyond literacy. It nurtures imagination, strengthens emotional bonds, and provides a screen-free activity that everyone can enjoy. By selecting engaging books, establishing a regular reading schedule, and incorporating interactive activities like acting out scenes or creating crafts, you can create a rich and rewarding storytelling tradition that brings your family closer together. These moments of shared stories not only foster learning but also create cherished memories and a deeper connection within your family.

Building a Family Culture of Communication

Open communication within a family is the cornerstone of trust and understanding. When you foster an environment where everyone feels comfortable expressing their thoughts and feelings, you lay the groundwork for a strong family bond. Open communication encourages emotional expression, allowing family members to share their joys, fears, and frustrations openly. This emotional transparency strengthens relationships and provides essential support during challenging times. Promoting open dialogue can help prevent misunderstandings and conflicts that often arise from assumptions or miscommunications. For instance, when a child feels heard and understood, they are less likely to act out, knowing they can discuss their concerns without fear of judgment or reprimand.

Creating safe spaces for communication is essential to nurturing this openness. Regular family meetings provide a structured opportunity for everyone to share their thoughts and feelings. These meetings can be informal, perhaps held weekly around the dinner table, where each person has the chance to speak without interruption. Encouraging active listening and empathy during these discussions is key. Teach your children to listen not just with their ears but with their hearts, aiming to understand the speaker's emotions and perspectives. Setting ground rules for respectful communication, such as not interrupting, using kind words, and respecting differing opinions, helps maintain a positive and supportive environment.

To further enhance communication skills within the family, consider incorporating specific techniques and activities. Practicing active listening exercises can be both fun and effective. For example, you could have one person speak for a set amount of time while the others listen without interrupting, followed by a discussion about what was heard and understood. Using "I" statements is another valuable tool to express feelings without assigning blame. Instead of saying, "You never listen to me," try saying, "I feel unheard when I'm interrupted." This approach reduces defensiveness and fosters more constructive conversations. Engaging in team- building activities or games can also strengthen communication. Games like "Feelings Charades," where players act out emotions, or "Communication Bingo," which involves completing tasks that require clear communication, can make learning these skills enjoyable.

Regular check-ins help maintain open lines of communication and ensure that everyone feels connected and supported. Establish daily or weekly "check-in" times to discuss the highs and lows of the day or week. These moments provide a platform for sharing experiences, celebrating successes, and addressing concerns. Keeping a family journal, where each member contributes thoughts and experiences, creates a shared narrative that reflects the family's journey together. Conversation starters can also help facilitate open dialogue during these check-ins. Questions like, "What was the best part of your day?" or "Is there anything you're worried about?" can guide the conversation and ensure everyone has a chance to speak.

Interactive Element: Communication Techniques Checklist

1. **Active Listening**: Practice listening without interrupting.

2. **"I" Statements**: Express feelings without blame.

3. **Family Meetings**: Establish regular times for open dialogue.

4. **Respectful Communication**: Set and follow ground rules.

By fostering open communication, creating safe spaces for dialogue, and incorporating regular check-ins, you can build a family culture where everyone feels heard and supported. This foundation of trust and understanding will strengthen your family bonds and equip your children with the communication skills they need to navigate their relationships and the world beyond your home. These habits create an environment of empathy and connection, preparing your family to face challenges together while deepening the sense of unity and emotional resilience.

Ending

This chapter explored various ways to strengthen family bonds, from game nights to fostering open communication. These practices help reduce screen time, foster deeper connections, and create lasting memories. As we move forward, the next chapter will focus on balancing screen time with academic responsibilities and promoting a healthy digital lifestyle. Together, these strategies will help ensure your family maintains a well-rounded and connected life both online and offline.